KING PENGU

D1566578

DANGEROUS PLAY
Poems 1974–1984

Andrew Motion was born in 1952 and educated at Oxford, where he won the Newdigate Poetry Prize. From 1977 to 1980 he was a lecturer in English at the University of Hull, and he subsequently became editor of *Poetry Review*. He is now Poetry Editor at Chatto and Windus. He has published two critical studies: *The Poetry of Edward Thomas* (1980) and *Philip Larkin* (1982); three collections of poetry: *The Pleasure Steamers* (1978), *Independence* (1981) and *Secret Narratives* (1983); and in 1982 he co-edited, with Blake Morrison, *The Penguin Book of Contemporary British Poetry*. He was elected a Fellow of the Royal Society of Literature in 1983. In 1981 he won the Arvon/*Observer* Poetry Prize, and for *Dangerous Play* he was awarded the John Llewelyn Rhys Memorial Prize for 1984, the first time in twenty-two years that this prestigious literary award has gone to a collection of poetry.

Andrew Motion enjoys a considerable reputation for his poetry. *The Times Literary Supplement* described *Independence* as 'a work of vivid surfaces and considerable depth'; Peter Porter writing in the *Observer* said, '*Secret Narratives* is good news for all who believe that verse should never have surrendered its birthright of fiction to prose'; the *Financial Times* wrote of *Dangerous Play*, 'the arrangement of this collection . . . is a triumph, each section enhancing our understanding of what has gone before, demonstrating the internal coherence of his writing . . . a most impressive whole'; and *The Times Literary Supplement* reviewing *Secret Narratives* said, 'he is remarkable for the precision of his technique – particularly in relating speech rhythms to the line of verse and registering vivid physical impressions . . . a natural heir to the traditions of Edward Thomas and Ivor Gurney'.

ANDREW MOTION

DANGEROUS
PLAY

Poems 1974–1984

A KING PENGUIN

PUBLISHED BY

PENGUIN BOOKS

Penguin Books Ltd, Harmondsworth, Middlesex, England
Viking Penguin Inc., 40 West 23rd Street, New York, New York 10010, U.S.A.
Penguin Books Australia Ltd, Ringwood, Victoria, Australia
Penguin Books Canada Ltd, 2801 John Street, Markham, Ontario, Canada L3R 1B4
Penguin Books (N.Z.) Ltd, 182–190 Wairau Road, Auckland 10, New Zealand

First published by The Salamander Press 1984
Published in Penguin Books 1985

Printed and bound in Great Britain by
Cox & Wyman Ltd, Reading
Offset from Salamander Press edition
Typeset in Monotype Garamond

In Memoriam
C.G.M.
20 June 1928–20 November 1978

CONTENTS

6

Acknowledgements

I

OPEN SECRETS

'The first time father erupted that day
was at Florrie rolling the dustbins downhill
to their emptying-pit. From the upstairs landing
I saw him arms crossed with his dressing-gown's
dark green paisley swirled in the wind, and Florrie
scarlet, still half swiveled round to the litter
as if it surprised her, tattering out in a trail
of scrumpled tissues and newspapers onto the moor.

After dark in McDermot's barn at the usual time
she told me his other disaster: how he had taken
five shots that day to finish his stag, and the fifth
was fired by McDermot. McDermot went with him
as gillie, and afterwards had the stag to himself
for keeping quiet. If ever Florrie stopped talking
we heard it next door through the pineboard wall,
dribbling and pinging blood in a metal bucket.'

Just now, prolonging my journey home to you, I killed
an hour where my road lay over a moor, and made this up.
Florrie I sat on a grass-grown crumbling stack of peat
with the boy by her side, and as soon as she whispered
Come on. We've done it before, I made him imagine
his father garotting the stag, slitting the stomach
and sliding his hands inside for warmth. He was never
myself, this boy, but I know if I tell you his story
you'll think we are one and the same: both of us hiding
in fictions which say what we cannot admit to ourselves.

THE LETTER

If I remember right, his first letter.
Found where? My side-plate perhaps,
or propped on our heavy brown tea-pot.
One thing is clear—my brother leaning
across asking *Who is he?* half angry
as always that summer before enlistment.

Then alone in the sunlit yard, mother
unlocking a door to call *Up so early?*
—waving her yellow duster goodbye
in a small sinking cloud. The gate creaks
shut and there in the lane I am running
uphill, vanishing where the woodland starts.

The Ashground. A solid contour swept
through ripening wheat, and fringe
of stippled green shading the furrow.
Now I am hardly breathing, gripping
the thin paper and reading *Write to me.*
Write to me please. I miss you. My angel.

Almost shocked, but repeating him line
by line, and watching the words jitter
under the pale spidery shadows of leaves.
How else did I leave the plane unheard
so long? But suddenly there it was—
a Messerschmitt low at the wood's edge.

What I see today is the window open,
the pilot's unguarded face somehow
closer than possible. Goggles pushed up,
a stripe of ginger moustache, and his eyes
fixed on my own while I stand
with the letter held out, my frock blowing,

before I am lost in cover again,
heading for home. He must have banked
at once, climbing steeply until his jump
and watching our simple village below—
the Downs swelling and flattening, speckled
with farms and bushy chalk-pits. By lunch

they found where he lay, the parachute
tight in its pack, and both hands spread
as if they could break the fall. I still
imagine him there exactly. His face pressed
close to the sweet-smelling grass. His legs
splayed wide in a candid unshamable V.

After what felt like a lifetime of rent
I bought somewhere my own. But at once,
in less than a week, he was writing:
Dear Madam, I hope you won't mind—

we met when I sold you the house.
It was mine. I gave you the china tea.
I showed you the room where you told me
yes, you could write in that room.

In the home I have now they are cruel.
There are traitors—and spies. I am hoping
my doctor is kind, but what is he doing
to bring me my wife, or give me her news?

Please, if this reaches you, tell her. Say—
if a visit is difficult, letters are fine.
Think of me reading this through at my desk,
throwing it down on my typewriter, frowning,

and wondering was this the room where she died?
Then think of my whisper to answer him:
Dearest heart. Forgive me. I'm ill
and dictating this. But I long for you always,

and when I'm recovered, I'll visit you.
Lazily spinning the phrases out, and finally
writing them, telling myself it was
kindness, and might even turn into love.

THE GREAT MAN

It was straight out of Conrad but true.
At mid-day I rounded the umpteenth turn
of the river, and there was the man himself,
surprised in the hospital yard. Just as I thought,
he was all I had never expected—far older,
no sign of the famous moustache, and the walk
a frightened scamper towards the jungle,
one hand cramming a yellow hat hard down.

He returned and was smiling, of course,
for the evening meal. *You are a journalist?*
Wonderful. Wonderful yes. And have taken a week?
To be with us? Or get here? Never you worry.
Someone will show you the hospital soon—
he is a pride and joy. If it were now,
I could not remember the clammy weight
of his hand on my shoulder more clearly,
half welcoming, half for support. Or the way
his eyes were scanning my face but staring
at someone else. Whoever it was appeared again
when he played—which was done like a maestro:
theatrical strides to the dais when supper was over,
and servants dragging his masterpiece centre-stage.

A rickety, straight-up, knee-hole, bamboo organ.
I knew about this. I had read in the books
how natives would 'gratefully leave their hearths
and listen enchanted for hours'. But I never imagined
he might have performed like a drain. He fumbled
through most of a fugue, steadfastly fixing his gaze
on the someone or something I could not see,

then the rain drowned him—beginning at sunset
like clockwork, and sullenly pounding the metal roof.

It never let up until morning. Lying in bed
I could follow a handful of patients prowling their ward
from window to window—glistening torsos and heads
as long as the power held out, and afterwards
abstract blurs. But just to be there was a cure,
everyone knew. Wasn't the doctor so gentle
he even avoided the ant which crossed his path?
How much he did for the dying, I would find out,
tagging along on his rounds with my camera poised.
Master. Master. You are a god to us. That was the woman
we found next day in the yard—the first of dozens.
She drew back the shawl from her raspberry shoulders
with almost a smile, but the doctor was shaking his head.
He prayed, which he always did, then ordered a poultice
of warm riverbank mud to be bound on her skin.

If I had said he was fake, who would have listened?
I was a stranger, and strangers were not to be trusted.
Do nothing, was all I could think. *When you are home,
then say whatever you like.* Well, here I am home today
—with my notebook and photographs spread on my desk,
and the rain which has blanketed London this morning
creasing my windows. Its whisper is scarcely a sound,
but it softens the stop-go scratching my pencil makes:
*He must have been eighty by then, but the moment
our ramshackle steamer nosed in by the jetty, there he was
striding to greet us, crushing my hand in his grip.*

2

INDEPENDENCE
(*for Alan Hollinghurst*)

A month home and awake
at three expecting light.
Still half the world in darkness
to roll away—but here I am

by the window, stooping,
quickly smearing a hole
in the misted silvery glass.
Your father's house,

his view of sand dunes
stubbled with grass, and the sea
heavily sliding, its craters split
and slammed shut to the moon.

As I look, wind staggers
the garden lilac, then races off
distressing the whole front—
the neighbour's gate squeaking

and banging, the pub-sign
knocking its frame once, twice,
and silent. But who is awake?
I glance at my bed and the sheet

thrown back, a crumpled ghost
where I slept—on the right,
as we did together. And there
with no more than the thought

I turn to the window again
and imagine you walking towards me—
in silence, bringing the friends,
the lost company, the servants I left,

everyone bowed and shawled
as though it were dawn, and this
wavering grey moonlight the dust
they had churned into early mist.

*

It was dawn when my journey finished
at last—three days, three nights stop-go
in my rickety Austin, a terrified
slow sweep from the Punjab down
past Delhi, Agra, Kanpur to reach

Kamaria: jumbled roofs and the sun
just clear into perfect blue. I drove
along sleeping streets, unshaven,
still scared. But no sign of the riots,
just slogans splashed and dribbling

Partition. No to Partition. Quit India.
What of my home? Would it be looted
by then? Or what? The manager's voice
came back to me over and over, blustering
Now we are free. No Britishers.

Now you must go—but smiling,
shaking my hand. Then I was home
and my servant ran to greet me:
Go, sahib, It is dangerous. Go.
All I could save was with me—

one suitcase, Shakespeare, a china mug
and the Hindustan Times, three days old.
I can see it now—your father's advertisement
circled with red ink, his name the friend
of a friend of a friend. In a week

when I stood in his narrow hall
for my interview, early, rehearsing my lines,
you were there. A sudden unthinking
surprised rush from your room, from a shower,
your hair darkened with water

and plastered down, your feet bare,
and one hand pulling the throat
of your dressing-gown close, hiding
the quick freckled blush I saw beginning
and deepening there like a burn.

*

So it began—our first blue midwinter.
Each cavernous cloudless morning
I drove to the godown at six

stocktaking wool for an hour:
indigo, crimson, natural, gold.
Then away round the villages—

Yes, I am new. Yes. Namaste.
The carpet sahib. Carpets—
and trained as an engineer . . .

House by house I ducked
and entered those close mud rooms.
The silences there. Fathers and sons

on their worn logs, smiling
through taut bars of string.
The twang and rustle of wool,

and the patterns rising.
Finish how soon? More smiles,
the waggling side-to-side head-shake,

Goodbye, and as evening approached
I circled back to my bungalow.
Would you be there? If I came

from Mirzapur, east, it was over
the high Ganges bridge. I would stop
midway, and leaning warily out

from the delicate parapet, whisper
your name *Let her love me.*
If not, let me not be found out.

Let her father like me. I waited
a moment, gazing down in the twilight,
then crumpled a single rupee note

and dropped it, straining to watch,
but never seeing the fall to its end
on the river's dark sluggish green.

*

It was our first time. We had shuffled
and clutched at club dances, and once
after tennis I kissed you, my hand
finding the warm small of your back,
brushing its damp soft hackle of hair.

Then it was midnight, and over the wall
I dropped down to the hushed MacFarlane garden—
your nervous adoring commando, crashing
and farcical. Which was your room?
Third right, in your letter. *Oh please,*

please come soon. I've been well
for at least ten days. My appendix is snug
in its jar on the window-sill, staring me out.
Your shutter unstuck with a parched squeak
Is it you? Yes. I kissed you again,

missing your mouth. *Ssssh.* The deliberate
firm tap-tapping of footsteps outside—
Nurse. Quick, in there, and I dragged
the heavy tallboy door shut behind me.
Your voices were hushed. *No, nothing*

thank you. Nothing. I'm fine. Good-night.
But I waited, your nightdress hanging
close to my face, silky, and smelling of talc.
Then I was out. *Shoes off*, you said. *That's all*,
and I eased myself down on your narrow bed.

Careful! My stitches. Lie still,
still as you can. Like this. On your back.
And so you unbuttoned me,
gingerly kneeling astride, and then
with that stealthy quickening dip and rise

you tipped evenly backwards and forwards
as if you were riding drunk—dissolving
the bed, the tallboy, the room, the dark coat
I ripped on the wall when I scrambled home
but wore unmended for days, as our secret sign.

*

Courting all that spring
to Independence—spring
and into the heat: shimmering days
I hurried to end for you.

Each late afternoon
we were side by side
at your father's bungalow,
longing for sunset, the punkah

lightly weighing us down
with its soft rush of air.
He smiled. *Really, you two.*
Go on . . . Supper's not yet . . .

24

and we were away, hand in hand
on the Austin's crackled back seat,
the windows open, our driver's face
staring ahead in the mirror.

They were perfect,
those cool evening drives:
the sun bleary with dust,
white eucalyptus avenues,

tiny flickering fires
and the sweet woodsmoke rising.
When will you marry me? Soon?
When you said it, you said it

lazily, breathing warm in my ear,
on that pot-holed road
out beyond Mirzapur. *Soon?*
We were late, with the engine off

at the crossing—a slender pole
waist high, and heat
still bouncing up from the rails,
warping the air. The keeper

emerged from his shack,
half lifted the pole,
listened, then slammed it back.
Up-down. Up-down you said, blushing,

and chafed my hand. We waited
in silence, hearing the train's deep
flustering *chomp, chomp* closer
and closer, a shrieking whistle,

and there it was. *Benares*—
Lahore on chipped plates,
windows barred, and the packed
vanishing faces of refugees.

*

Married in Independence week.
The factory shut, and the church
packed with the carpet wallahs
who caught us up in their holiday.
Now we are free, they were shouting,

Free—roping our necks with garlands
of roses and gainders. That night
before taking our honeymoon journey
north to the hills, we were secret
in Mirzapur's ramshackle best hotel,

strolling late round the pool.
A three foot scummy drop
to the water—its glassy length
steady and speckled with insects
performing their tiny pointless dance,

with the last swimmer long gone.
*I love you. Look at us. Husband
and wife*—you pointed down
at our faces, stared, and turned inside,
Come on—leaving your hand still grasped

in mine as we reached for the key
and the snub black light-switch.
Then you were screaming—*Let go*.
A furious quick sizzle. *Let go*. *Let go,*
and I did, with a sticky tear of skin.

We were driving at once, my good right hand
tight on the wheel, your left stretched
over, changing the gears to MacFarlane.
Back here—you said it teeth clenched
as we stood in the dark porch

side by side for a moment,
our hands held out before us.
You nodded towards them: *Well?*
Well—nothing, I said, and smiled
leading you in. *Nurse? Hello? Are you there?*

*

A month alone
but stirring slowly, making
room in our lives for news

outside ourselves. Spring
brought the heat again—day
after day in my office the papers

built rustling under their weights,
shaken and plucked as the punkah
whipped round in its clammy rush.

On my wall I had pinned the first
free replacement map—India,
Pakistan: the new word jagged

up through the Indus valley to end
in the mountains' lumpy bruise.
When Gandhi died, your father

traced the frontier down
saying *Now. Now we shall see,*
and bowed his head, suddenly

homesick for England. Next day
he was round the villages talking,
cajoling, then back at my desk

empty-handed. *It's grief,* he said.
They won't do anything. You understand.
He stared at my map and sighed,

imagining high white cliffs
and gantries clearing through mist—
a dockside glossy with early rain.

*

With your father gone, and his furniture
gone or stacked in the godown waiting,
the house was ours. Tall white-washed rooms
and the spaces he left: dents in a carpet

for chairs, the crushed square of a cupboard.
Take care, he said, with his brave face
in the cabin doorway. *Remember,*
as soon as the baby comes, write.

Soon as you can. Now please . . . But we stayed
all morning, staring up from the quay,
scanning the rails for his wave
and seeing nothing, then nothing again

when he sailed, the liner unthinkably huge
as they tugged it clear, but suddenly
tiny—a slow dispersing feather
of smoke spiralling north. We imagined it

fading for days—free with ourselves
to ourselves at last. Each night
was our tender private game. *Listen.*
What can you hear? You would be lying back

with your dress pulled up, holding
my head side-on to your stomach. *Anything?*
Yes. I craned for the child's gurgle—
Yes. A boxer. That or a football player.

We slept outside that summer,
two wide-eyed effigies hand in hand
on the cool veranda, our hearts racing,
watching the stars blaze and swing

away through our nets. Five months,
six, and then for a week my trip alone
to Delhi on business. Should you have come?
Was that it? Even in summer? I travel

the last few miles of the journey back
endlessly. There is the taxi again
almost home from the station, and there
am I, with the windows wound right down

so my eyes run, blurring the house
and the one servant who met me.
Where is the memsahib? My question
returns off dazzling white walls. *Sahib*

he says, in a deep widening silence.
I remember cicadas, their manic bowing,
and sun crashing up from the yard,
then his voice breaks, *O Sahib*

and he turns towards me weeping.
But I am refusing to understand,
grinning, thinking of nothing
and letting the same unbidden phrase

occur to me over and over. *Sahib*—
he says it again. *I show you now.*
Humpti-tumpti gir giya phat.
Humpti-tumpti gir giya phat.

*

A scar of yellow clods.
The scratchmark of something
vanished. A dry scuffle.
You will wake up,
I was thinking, *Wake up,*

crouched with my head tilted
sideways as if I might
just make out your voice.
Sahib. It was the servant,
still weeping. *Baba too soon*

and bad. Like a snake.
I was hardly listening,
lost in the first moment
I brought you to life
underground: your hair set,

powder soft on your cheek,
and the dress slinking
back from your bare arms
as you stretch and show me
our slippery mottled child.

*

My solaces. The day's long
self-forgetting work, embarrassed
by those sad half-shouts
above the punkah whirring

Can I help you sahib?
Then evenings drunk alone—
the bedroom shutters drawn
and my shadow reeling to

and fro across their slats
folding dresses into tea-chests,
scooping up the baby-things,
your belts, a lacy petticoat,

shoes, blouses from the cupboard.
So much of you to find—
three nights but always something
overlooked, and then a fourth,

and rain. Almost home, I was
head-down through the yard
and stifling when it broke.
A long-drawn sizzling rip

like linen tearing, then
a pause and then the first
big drops, distinct and smashed
in puffing spurts of dust.

Monsoon again. That night
I stretched across our bed
and drank among your last
unsorted clothes, the houselights

all turned off. No sleep,
but blankness interrupted
suddenly to find the rain
had quickened, thunder

cannoning above my roof,
the eucalyptus shimmering
and thrashed—its whole
enormous height smoking

in a constant crash.
Then blankness swimming back,
the rain dissolving,
and a dream releasing me

beyond my room, my garden,
bobbing on a grey race
of water to your grave.
I scrambled deep beside you

and was dry, tugging
at your clothes, whispering
Let go. Give me these
for laundry. Let them go.

                    *

How many days? Two, three, I let myself
sink from the world, half sleeping
or dreaming awake, with the rain
a steady hissing downpour, seething
to rot me through. When I first stood

outside in the glittering yard
it was morning. A week? More,
since you died? Nobody said—
it was all *Come here, sahib.*
Come quick, and someone splashing

ahead to the compound gates. *There.*
They waved one arm, its arc
sweeping the whole slope: *Ganga.*
I thought of your grave buried
deep underwater, and with it

the whole plain to my feet—
fields and dusty tracks lost
in a dimpled yellow-green lake
where bloated cattle were drifting
twice their size, gable ends

jutted from froth, and the trees
had grown astonishing packages—
carpets rolled and strung above water,
their dark sacks a roost
for files of sodden ridiculous birds.

                          *

Now sit, sahib. Sit here.
It was the holy man,
patting the veranda floor.

Good. His face caked white
and crouched body
draped in a leopard skin—

a circus strongman
reading my life. *Sahib.*
You are an educate man.

Don't be afraid.
I am educate too: Hazlitt.
The beautiful lake poets.

You are lonely.
Eyes closed, and the greasy
ropes of hair. One hand pressing

down on his wire cage
and its parrot—a brilliant
green hat-feather tail.

You are lonely now.
His mesmerised voice
pausing, collecting itself.

You must go.
Your work here, finished.
The factory, finished,

his head leant sideways
and then *No more*—
almost a shout.

These are your own thoughts.
He was gone—
a faltering stooped prance

down to the yard, dragging
one leopard's foot in the dust.
Did I dream it?

Lying before me
were grains of wheat, a twig,
a charred thick chupatty.

*

My life out of my hands. By autumn
two, perhaps three carpets a week.
Never enough. When I drove out
the weavers' houses were empty
ruinous shells, looms unstrung,

and everyone working all day in the fields,
shovelling grey Ganges silt into banks,
scraping and patting their ditches.
They will come back to us.
That was Pradeep, swirling his drink

as our final December AGM
dragged on. He frowned, *But when?*
They must care for their land . . .
then a shrug, and a blank stare
outside to the compound walls

and still eucalyptus trees.
We shall see. Yes, we shall see.
We spoke without thinking,
leaving the date of our sale
still vague as the evening darkened

and *Well*, said Pradeep, relieved
and embarrassed. *Well, we must finish*.
Time we should change. For the party
he meant—Mirzapur Christmas Dance
at the Club. By ten I was there, drunk

and hearing The Inkspots *Bless you*
for being an angel. Bless you for making
a new world just when the old world
crumbled so help-less-ly. The record
again and again like a commonplace

tender grief for that sweltering room
with its swathes of tinsel and ivy,
its yellow billiard cloths, and its walls
dotted with cotton-wool glued there
by servants who had never seen snow.

*

I woke at five to a bare house,
luggage already half way home.
My last morning: a delicate stripe
of sky strengthening under my door

and the chowkidar's shadowy steps
backwards and forwards, his cough,
and the phlegm with its soft scatter.
When I looked out he was gone—

his charpoy tipped to the wall,
and a torn-off tooth-brush stick
thrown on the balcony steps.
Sahib. A voice loud in the hall.

The driver's come.
I was bowed in the cold yard
as the servants draped their garlands on.
Roses and gainders—a necklace

of sweet-smelling tickling loops.
Goodbye, sahib. Goodbye. Goodbye.
I salaamed to the puckered faces,
not daring to speak, and was blind

through the compound gates and on
for a mile, two, of the dusty lane
until I leant forward. *Stop. Wait for me,
wait,* and I knelt at your grave.

Then the memory blurs. I can follow
my tentative hand to your stone,
touching as if it were braille—
Beloved wife. Their child,

but the images shift, and here I am
almost asleep at the window again,
smearing a hole in its misted
silvery glass. There are footsteps now—

your father's, crossing the landing.
He calls to me, *Seven o'clock,*
and the bathroom door squeaks.
I watch a milkfloat clattering

house by house down the street,
and daylight begin. The sun is no more
than a thin whitening slit. The sea
a bleak horizon returning to grey.

3

ANNE FRANK HUIS

Even now, after twice her lifetime of grief
and anger in the very place, whoever comes
to climb these narrow stairs, discovers how
the bookcase slides aside, then walks through
shadow into sunlit rooms, can never help

but break her secrecy again. Just listening
is a kind of guilt: the Westerkirk repeats
itself outside, as if all time worked round
towards her fear, and made each stroke
die down on guarded streets. Imagine it—

three years of whispering and loneliness
and plotting, day by day, the Allied line
in Europe with a yellow chalk. What hope
she had for ordinary love and interest
survives her here, displayed above the bed

as pictures of her family; some actors;
fashions chosen by Princess Elizabeth.
And those who stoop to see them find
not only patience missing its reward,
but one enduring wish for chances

like my own: to leave as simply
as I do, and walk at ease
up dusty tree-lined avenues, or watch
a silent barge come clear of bridges
settling their reflections in the blue canal.

THE PLEASURE STEAMERS

It's blowing cold from the east,
but still, they're working tonight
on the steamers, more shadows than men:
each canvas peels back like a chrysalis,

benches are turned to the view
in narrow saloons. It's as if I was
watching last summer restored. Or more
than last summer. The name picked out

in lights from the bridge is one
my father saw, lying offshore
in 1940, from France—*Mapledurham*
dark red for safety, and home.

Soon I'll take his place.
And though I've no danger
of dying, without his cause,
I'll look from the varnished deck

like him, not searching
for what I expect, but what I need:
cities reduced to innocent wharves; punts
moored over their image in obsolete pastoral.

*

The river repeats itself, and I
repeat myself watching it; here is
my hand on the bridge as it was
this morning, and here in a crevice

of moss the match I dropped then.
Everything waits for me till I live
far enough forward to find it changed:
now what I see in the twilight

as logs, rotate on the current
as sluggish and matted as what
I guessed must have been hidden
early today. There was a van

drawn up by the rushes, and on the mud
a diver, easing his mask off,
calling *I couldn't see anything*.
Neither could I. Just clouds

on indolent stretches of water,
and somewhere beneath it
an absence of light, increasing,
billowed towards me like dust.

*

The steamers are ready:
one by one their lights go
out in the water, and in a day
they'll take up summer stations.

How can I help but admire
their implacable constancy?
Year after year I see them
leaving like gaudy ghosts

with nowhere to haunt
but their past. Defeats
and drownings have never
prevented their journey,

and now they're caught
in a separate world, sailing
for ever from here to the end
of a lost, inexhaustible century

where I may sometimes visit
but never stay, although
I discover at every return
I could have outlived myself there.

LEAVING BELFAST
(*for Craig Raine*)

Driving at dusk on the steep road
north to the airport, *Look back,*
you say, *The finest view of Belfast,*
and point, proud of your choice to stay.

How clear the rows of streetlamps show
which way we came. I trace them slope
by slope through marshlands slipping down
to lanes, and find the roofs again,

their stern geographies of punishment
and love where silence deepens under rain.
Each sudden gust of light explains itself
as flames, but neither they, nor even

bombs redoubled on the hills tonight
can quite include me in their fear.
What does remains invisible, is lost
in curt societies whose deaths become

revenge by morning, and whose homes
are nothing more than all they pity most.
I watch the moon above them, filling rooms
with shadow politics, though whether

voices there pronounce me an intruder,
traitor, or a friend, I leave them now
as much a stranger as I came, and turn
to listen in the twilight for their griefs,

but hear instead the promise of conclusion
echoing towards me through these miles
of stubborn gorse, until it disappears
at last in darkness, out beyond the coast.

FROM THE IMPERIAL
Kerkyra

Now I am almost asleep
and the hotel is locked,
whose is this voice,
this dream companion
dead a century ago?

He lives as I imagine—
Edward Lear, lonely
and bigongulous, wishing
he were an egg. I watch him
climbing dark stairs

towards a room like mine,
and drawing shutters tight
on moonlight fallen
jiggy-jaggy in the bay.
Such fragrant darknesses.

Such secrecy. From night
to night he keeps himself
without a word for love,
and then sails north
at last, his boat weighted

down with chairs, tables,
and an upright black piano
strapped and locked on deck,
the varnish quickly warming
as it flashes back the sun.

BEGINNING THE MOVE

The day I began my move, they happened
to fly the wounded home. I would have been
hands on hips by the bookshelves wondering
Where do I start? as the first plane
crescendoed and wheeled away to the country—
a VC 10 set for our toytown local base.

I soon forgot it—toing and froing
with armfuls of books, first, then clothes,
then jittery plates. But in mid-afternoon,
when I was almost done, and just dizzily
mooning down aisles of loaded tea-chests,
the plane returned out of nowhere, huge,

and filling my mind's eye once more.
I imagined it parked at Arrivals, engines off,
but still with their rippling trumpets of air,
and a door was gaping wide at the wing
where the soldiers appeared: on stretchers,
some hobbling, some with arms round friends

like drunks helped towards bed, and one—
why did he look Chinese?—emerging at last
in tears, with a pantomime sliding stagger.
Before he was off the steps he had vanished,
lost with the rest as a hectic crush
of families jostled me back to myself.

By then I was through to the kitchen,
and found I was slouched with my face leant
close to the goldfish tank, watching the fish
wriggle and flick in the cave of my silhouette,
and my mouth relaxing a comical kneading pout
to ask aloud *How shall I ever move you?*

4

THE WHOLE TRUTH

When I missed the mid-day boat to you
what I saw were theatre tricks: a funnel
skimming on trees, and the chattering deck
now here now gone in a cloud of thorn.

But that was all right. Three hours
to wait strolling the island were hours
to be thinking of you. On the stage in my head
you were slouched at your kitchen table,

check shirt with the sleeves rolled up,
thick hair in your eyes, half-watching
the hazy sun on your garden outside:
a brown iron fence and broken roller

both turned by the light into nothing
like substance, yet visibly scaled with dew.
The way I was looking, I knew you were
thinking of me, wondering *Where is he now?*

and deciding *The boat*—seeing my hands
on the flaking rail, face grey in the wind,
and miniature islands slithering past
like knots in the wood-coloured sea.

And all of it lies, just as my pictures
of you at your kitchen table were lies—
one tender imaginary scene succeeding
another, but only to prove what is true.

Two hundred miles from home I found
the one lonely room where you live,
and that, as you said, was *Nothing,
really. Not even my own. See this?
It's Madame Dussart's funeral gown,
filling a whole drawer. Supposing
I died first, of boredom, what then?*

Then nothing again. A vacant room
where no one would see the sunlight
mark time in dust towards your bed.
As if we were ghosts of ourselves
we waited for darkness, watching it
deepen to bring us together again
like shadows, our close definition.

And shadows we stated, or tried to,
knowing, before it fell, that night
after night would discover us still
caught in our absolute lives. If not
the room, what was there outside to blame,
hidden except when headlights below
reminded us where they travelled towards?

Vimy, Arras, Bapaume: I imagined
the brilliant signs, whitening south
through your country of maps and towns
in history. Nothing escaped itself—
not even the wind, tracing a ridge
of lost lines over the fields, always
raising the same delicate spray of graves.

They were complete societies, flickering
stones I knew by distant village names.
However I chose I remembered them,
all preserved no matter what deaths
succeeded them there, and us, who talking
each other to sleep at last heard only
their luminous silence we could not survive.

THESE DAYS

It might be any night
these days, when every night
is like nothing on earth.
Tired with drinking, we long

for your riotous children
to wear themselves out
and shamble off to their beds.
Make it be soon, my eyes say

rolling up to the ceiling—
a relished, leisurely roll
which tells you as well
I want you. Bowing low

so your forehead rests
on the rumpled table-cloth
just for a second, you pour
milk in a shallow dish

for the cat, as he frisks in
out of nowhere, his hollow
lap-lap-lapping an almost
welcome distraction to stop me

pining for you, his tongue
steadily clearing the milk
like a tiny frog, revealing
a woman crossing a blue bridge

setting out on a journey,
perhaps, or coming back,
her parasol raised in salute,
her blue cross-hatched hat

tipped to deflect the wind,
and her eyes distinctly narrowed
to blue expressionless flecks
by a sudden onrush of light.

COMING TO VISIT

Your daughter Kate saw the ghost
the same summer night your twin
came for her visit. I had been happy,
before, always to leave you alone
for the twin to talk to you late,
but this time something was wrong.

In the bedroom, staring down
at the single acacia and beech
which suddenly loomed like a wood,
I was willing the close-set leaves
to obscure me, to let me be lost
to the world and everyone in it.

I should have said I was jealous
and nothing else, but whatever
the reason, I slipped myself out
through the oiled front door
to the trees—where the wind
was hissing like rain in a fire—

then the river beyond. There,
when I had danced my way over nettles
down to the mossy bank, and struck
—as anyone would have admitted—
a precious, theatrical pose,
I could almost be sure I believed

a double was what I was missing.
You and your twin swam deftly
into my head, side by side asleep
as if you were children, linking
your warm, brown, identical arms
and breathing each others' breath.

All I could actually see, though,
was my head in the water distorted
half by ripples, half by the moon,
so it seemed I was watching a head
appear in a well, or a rocky cleft,
which might—if I ever allowed it—

give itself gnomic, oracular airs.
I imagined a gravelly voice,
of course: *Whoever loves best
loves best by remaining themselves*
— something I more or less knew
in my heart, and then knew in fact

when a light blazed on behind me
and Kate, with a panicky shout,
was calling your name. In her room,
absurdly soaked to the knees
where I had scrambled through waves
of dripping grass, I found you

already beside her, stretched
on her jangly, brass-headed bed
hugging her close, and Kate—
whispering into your shoulder
as if she were shy, or ashamed—
explaining not just how the ghost

must have watched her sleeping,
but how when she woke she discovered
one freckled arm had been slithered
subtly over her shoulder, the better
to ease her onto her side, and the face,
staring an inch from her face, was her own.

5

SKATING

I am peering through a fringe of white silk tassels. There is a sun, but it is low and cold. Occasionally a warm shadow blots it out, looming down to my face with a smell of what I will come to recognise as *Blue Grass*. The shadow is my mother, and she is pushing me in my pram on a frozen mill pond. If I concentrate, I can hear the sharp hiss of her skates, and the duller scrape of my pram wheels skidding, not turning, over the ice. The mill house itself is hidden behind us, but the pond is clear enough: a white half-acre fringed with floppy reeds, and the wreck of a swan's nest tucked into the bank on my left. There is the O of a water rat's hole beside it, and a miniature something (in time I will know it is a union jack) is sticking out of the hole on a metal rod. The flag is frozen in a stiff extended flutter.

But this is a photograph. I've seen it in one of the albums my father keeps in my mother's desk. I have forgotten the afternoon on the mill pond completely—or maybe I was too young when it occurred to realise that it ever existed. Nevertheless, it endures in my mind's eye as one of my earliest memories, along with other memories which are in fact photographs. In one I am the pudgy, grinning baby who could be anyone, sprawling on a tartan rug outside the house my parents bought after the mill. (I was threatening to walk, and the mill became dangerous. The new house was a dark Victorian warren called Little Brewers, which was apt: my father was a brewer.) In another photograph someone has dumped me in a forest of cowparsley and I am trying to escape. It's only the garden again, but the image freezes me on the edge of tears, tottering towards the camera through confusing, monstrously-ribbed stems.

*

I can remember very little of my childhood. Why? 'Life is first boredom, then fear,' Philip Larkin tells us, but since I became conscious, I've always thought that he put it the wrong way round. For me—at least since I was sent away to school—life has been first fear and then the fear of boredom. And fear (of doing badly at work, of being bullied) meant that my school-days passed in a cringing inattentiveness. Holidays, by contrast, were blissfully contented—so absolutely so that their details have also dissolved into an almost-featureless haze. The few actual memories which stand out refuse to form themselves into the impressionistic rush which seems to be the usual experience of childhood. They survive, instead, as random snapshots, separated by long blanks. I was made vague, alternately, by beauty and by fear. Significantly (I suppose) one of my earliest definite recollections is standing in my bedroom at Little Brewers when I was seven, just before prep-school began, staring into the garden with my forehead against the window, thinking 'Up to now life has been all holidays with occasional bouts of term. Now it's going to be all term with occasional bouts of holiday.' The only abiding thing, linking these isolated moments and suffusing the nothings between them, was the sense of my mother.

*

What did she look like? Very beautiful. 5 foot 8½ inches ('I could always have joined the police force') with fair hair a bit darker than mine. When I brushed her hair, I had to be careful that the bristles didn't strike the large mole at her crown. This mole used to embarrass her, and the hair would be brushed over it in a long wave. There was a mole on her cheek, too, and you could feel its soft bump when she kissed you. One nostril was slightly lifted where she had hit her nose falling off a pony. These things used to worry me when I was a child: my brother Kit (who is two years younger than me) and I both thought that they 'spoilt' her. Now they seem to make her more perfect by making her more human. But we were always proud of the way she looked, and enjoyed it. We used to creep into her bed in the morning, as soon as my father had gone off to work. 'You're no good,' she'd tell me. 'You're a lamp-post.' (I was hopeless at cuddling.) Then she would dress while we lay and watched her. When she was finished, and the hair-brushing began, she would sit at her kidney-shaped dressing table. It had a glass top, and underneath this she had slipped photographs of my father, my brother and myself. You could see the photographs over her shoulder: me in my pram on the mill pond; me in the forest of cowparsley. My vanity and hers were appeased at one and the same time.

*

Before prep-school was a day school. I can hardly remember it at all. There was the time I entered a singing competition (bravely as I thought; foolishly as it turned out) and humiliated myself by coming last. 'Imagine there's a fairy on the clock at the back of the hall,' my mother said. 'Then you won't get nervous.' But it didn't work. I was literally sick with relief when it was all over. And there was the tarmac playground, ruled by Malcolm, where you could easily graze your knees.

But prep-school, when it came, was unimaginably worse. When I think about it now, my memories demand that I protect myself by rehearsing them as anecdotes, not as sensory experiences. Although much more painful events were to occur in later life, I don't seem to need to be so defensive about them: I feel, rightly or wrongly, that I can control them. But at prep-school I felt that I had no control—no say in how I ordered my life, or expressed and explained it to myself.

Because I'd never doubted for a second that my parents adored me, I never really believed that they would send me away. How did they imagine we could live apart? What was the point? If they did try to explain, I have forgotten. (Their friends' children went away to school—that was probably all it was.) Before they left, they pushed me into the company of an older boy I knew vaguely from home. 'You're a Jap,' he said. 'And I'm the Allied Forces,' then chased me round the hall. I was crying so bitterly I could scarcely see where I was going. But when I stopped, and dried my eyes, I looked through the double glass doors which led from the hall to the vestibule, and there was my mother looking in, crying too.

The school was a sandstone Victorian country house with peculiar lead-capped towers at its four corners. The headmaster was a friend and contemporary of my grandfather's. This meant that the remoteness he had as a teacher was slightly diminished, but I don't think he ever took any special interest in me. His real passion was orchids, and in season the grounds would suddenly become exotic with bizarre blooms. We thought they were rather disgusting, since they reminded us of him. The grounds themselves were large and full of mystery: The Wilderness (a huge—though probably in fact quite small—evergreen wood); Dinkey Farm (a slithery pit where we played with our toys); and The Lake (full of golden orfe and crossed by stepping-stones which only prefects were allowed to use). There were games every afternoon, and I was good at them. From the age of about ten I could run faster than anyone in the school, and this gave me a sense of identity. I traded on it—in a mildly tyrannical way—to the extent that I formed a gang, and on Wednesday and Sunday afternoons (when we had 'Muck-About' and no games) we used to run futilely round the grounds looking for things to do. We also dug a large hole in The Wilderness, roofed it with planks and covered the planks with earth, and called it The Hut. When we weren't running around, we'd retreat to The Hut and smoke pine needles wrapped up in lavatory paper.

So outdoors was more or less all right. It was a haven from indoors, where I had no feeling of purpose or ability, and where whatever successes I'd had at games never helped me. If I'd been unsure of myself at work before I arrived, my nervousness was rapidly intensified by my first teacher, Miss Hangwick. She was tall, grey, and generally considered to be 'a good sort'. But her secret vice, when we disappointed her, was to inflict on us the 'Haggie Hairpull'. Rogers, whose hair came out very easily, was virtually scalped one afternoon. I can still see the large hank in Miss Hang-wick's hand.

I can also see now that Miss Hangwick had a tiresome and thwart-ing life. But in those days (most children have so little sense of adults' cares and responsibilities) I simply disliked her. She made me feel stupid, and feeling stupid made me feel—and be—wet. I looked like a cissy, too, with my fair hair, and I was clearly spoilt by my mother. She sent me, during my first term (twelve weeks long) twenty-six parcels—usually plastic model kits of ships. One Sunday afternoon a group of boys led me outside, took off my shirt, tied me to a cedar tree, and beat me with bamboo canes. I still have the scars on my back—but I don't remember ever telling my mother. I wanted to be a success for her.

Being able to run fast was never really enough. I simply couldn't find any work to do well. By the time I moved on from Miss Hang-wick, every subject was terrifying—in my dormitory I kept a bible on my bedside chair and slept with one hand holding on to it. 'Please God,' I'd pray, 'let me see the light.' Latin and Maths were especially bad: I cheated as hard as I could, and squeezed blood from my bitten finger-nails onto my prep, so that the person marking it could see I'd been making an effort. English was marginally prefer-able to other subjects—but only marginally. Spelling and précis were at least only dreary, not actually frightening, and writing essays could be fun, if the title was an exciting one like 'River In Flood', or 'How I Survived The Earthquake'. We rarely got round to writing or talking about poems, but we did occasionally have to learn them. I can still recite most of 'The chief defect of Henry King' and de la Mare's 'Nod'. They never meant much to me, though: poetry, everyone agreed, was for cissies. But if I was a cissy, why wasn't it for me? Oh well.

*

Nevertheless, during my last few holidays from prep-school, I found myself writing stories. (It was probably to curry favour.) They were giftless—melodramatic accounts of car accidents and Indian massacres—but I'd be pleased and surprised by them, and take them into my mother's bed in the morning to read them to her. 'Why are you so bloodthirsty?' she'd ask—and I'd never be sure whether this implied praise or blame. I can see now that the stories were ways of imagining the worst: ways of trying to prolong the idyll of her company by dreaming up some radically appalling alternative.

In fact the pleasures of holidays lasted for years, though their details are nearly all forgotten. We never did anything which might be construed as having the remotest connection with school work: no theatre, no art galleries, no concerts—we simply weren't interested. We were busily occupied, though: Little Brewers was (in those days) near unspoilt country, and we led a typical landed life. It was extremely horsey. Hunting dominated the winter, and in the summer my mother, Kit and I went for a long ride each morning. Kit was much more adventurous and proficient than I was; I think riding rather scared me. In the afternoon, my mother rested on her bed for an hour, and we never gave it a second thought. But the more I think about her now, the more mysterious her life seems. Did she feel catastrophically bored? She was often ill: was she appealing for more attention from us? What did she do when Kit and I weren't there? At the time, she seemed to exist entirely for us—after her rest she would walk the dogs with us, or go shopping with us, or come for a bike ride with us. She had a vast black upright bike, with what looked like a dead umbrella over the back wheel to stop mud splashing up. Once I threw a stick into the spokes as she was pedalling along, to see what happened. She fell off, of course. I think I must have thought she was infallible.

In my very earliest memories, my mother is just *there*: entirely trustworthy and always affectionate. But as I grew up, and became aware of her personality, I realised that I liked her very much, as well as loving her instinctively. She was brave, she was sensible, and she made me laugh. She also made me feel special by sometimes confiding in me as she might have done with an equal. I sensed that her character had exciting reserves which I would discover when I was older. Not that I spent any time articulating such things: when I was with her, I was much too busy enjoying myself. But I do deeply wish that I could now remember more actual incidents—like the time I stopped my pony in a wood, and discovered that I was eye-level with a pigeon on its nest. I can still see the ramshackle tangle of twigs, and the bird with its beautiful swollen crop and its wet eye staring me out.

When I read *White Fang* just before I left prep-school, I thought of the pigeon again, and wondered what it would be like to taste it. I think that was the first time a book related, more or less directly, to my own experience. Most books described a world which had nothing to do with me—hardly surprising in view of what I read. I had a craze for Dennis Wheatley, then Hammond Innes, then Alastair Maclean, and eventually Ian Fleming—who was considered rather risqué. I read *Casino Royale* for an hour and a half every Thursday afternoon when my mother was out having her hair done, and there was no fear of interruption. *Casino Royale* was a yellow-paged paperback, kept in the drawing room in a rotating bookstand known as 'the whirlygig'. 'The whirlygig' held most of my parents' books, and there wasn't space for many. My father used to say, laughing but almost-seriously, that all he had read was half *The Lonely Skier* (on holiday, but the holiday ended too soon for him to finish). This never seemed extraordinary, since he never had any time. He would leave for work at six in the morning, get home late and tired, then disappear most week-ends to 'play soldiers', as my mother said. He had stayed on in the T.A. after the war, and eventually commanded the Essex Yeomanry. Kit and I were very proud of that, but we didn't see a great deal of him. I can remember, night after night, the glowing end of his cigarette burning towards us through the dark when he came to kiss us good-night. 'Bristly!', Kit and I would complain, but we adored it. He smelt of smoke and London.

*

I expected my next school to be an X certificate version of prep-school, and to start with it seemed so. Everything I did was wrong. I wore a buttoned pull-over (a prefect's privilege); I walked on the grass (ditto); and—worst of all—I smiled at older boys (I was a tart). By the end of my first term, though, my teachers had convinced me that learning wasn't as intimidating as I'd always imagined, and I relaxed. In fact I even started to be quite good at some things— especially English, which consisted largely of writing essays (more rivers in flood and earthquakes), and reading the First World War poets (every English teacher in the school seemed to be addicted to them). Life outside the classroom started to brighten up, too: there was Chapel every day, which I enjoyed, and there was Social Hall. This was the large room that boys shared for their first year, everyone having a wooden enclave called a 'horsebox' where you kept your books and tuck, and did your work. The sort of camaraderie which prevailed in Social Hall was what I imagine the feeling must have been like in a Prisoner of War camp. It was 'us' against 'them', and even our most minor law-breakings generated a profound sense of community.

For the first time, I found myself distracted from the thought of home. I still longed for it, and for the two letters a week that my mother wrote me, but my homesickness lost that rubber-kneed, stomach-loosening intensity I'd almost always felt at prep-school. It was partly a matter of being more confident, and partly that for the first time I made a close friendship—with a boy called Sandy Nairne. Sandy made me think. It never occurred to me until years afterwards, but the fact that he came from a professional background whereas most of my previous acquaintances were from landed families—my prep-school was that kind of place—made an enormous difference to me. When I went to stay with him in the holidays, I joined a society where it was perfectly normal—indeed, it was the done thing—to talk about books and paintings and so on. Although Sandy never wrote poems himself—he drew very well— he encouraged me to feel that there was nothing peculiar about reading them.

Then I got arthritis, and spent most of a year at home: no Kit to compete with, my father away most of every day—just my mother and me together. It was wonderful, and I realise now that if it hadn't existed I would hardly have known her at all. By this time we had moved to a high-ceilinged, Georgian ex-rectory in north Essex. It was cut off from the lane by a thick belt of trees (mostly elms— they're dead now) and felt secluded and magical. For the first few months of my illness I had a bed made up downstairs, and through the window there was a huge chestnut tree. The lower branches had been rubbed smooth by the horses scratching their backs, and the bark was greasy and covered with hairs.

After her morning ride, my mother would sit with me, or potter about the house doing her chores. I lived her life vicariously: I could hear the radio and the crackle of cooking from the kitchen, and smell the dry almost-scorched ironing. I suppose she was denying herself whatever she normally did during term, but she never made me aware that I was a nuisance. I just felt loved and grateful. I also felt, in an accidental sort of way, included for the first time in an adult world which was usually disguised during the holidays proper. There was a large stone fireplace in my bedroom, and when my father came home from work, they'd sit by the fire with me between them. After they had gone to bed I'd watch the fire sinking in the darkness and listen to them undressing upstairs. It had never occurred to me before to ask myself whether they were happy together—now I could see that they were.

*

My mother and I never talked much about sex—I think she must have just wanted me to find out about it for myself. School—so I was led to believe—was full of people who had 'been the whole way' with girls, and it was difficult not to feel that one wanted to do it too. The best chance seemed to be with Caroline Coleridge, and after some unusually (for me) confident manoeuvrings at a party, I got what I wanted: an invitation to stay and go to a dance with her.

I was still about eighteen months away from learning to drive, so on these sort of occasions my mother would either take me herself, or put me on a bus. This time it was to be the bus. After breakfast I packed my case, ill with trepidation. Should I take Caroline a present?

70

There was a whole day together before the dance began: would we have anything to say to one another? Then my mother and I drove down the lane, through the village, down the long hill with its tunnel of trees, and up to the bus stop on the main road. It was December, with occasional blasts of snow, and an east wind was blowing. My mother was hunting with Kit later that day, and she was wearing a stock under her green jersey. We waited with the engine on, to keep the heater working. 'Have you got everything?' 'Yaaas,' said in that flat way we'd evolved, meaning 'don't flap'. 'Will you be all right?' 'Yaaaas.' When the bus came it was a double-decker. Without knowing why (why didn't I want to assert my independence?) I climbed to the top as quickly as I could and stared through the back window. I saw her car, the green Hillman estate, pull away from the bus stop and head for the lane home again. As she went, she bibbed her horn, and crouched right down to look up at me. She waved, and I waved, and the car turned out of sight.

Not much survives of my day with Caroline, but we got through it. By six-thirty I was in the spare-room, changing for the dance. It was a cosy, dark-panelled room, but the bed didn't look very big, and when I sat on it the springs gave a loud lunatic jangle. I tentatively bounced up and down, then stopped, guilty, when there was a knock on the door. 'It's Caroline with a plan,' I thought. But it wasn't. It was her mother.

When I think back over the next few minutes, they seem to be as clear as if I were living them now, and yet profoundly unreal—invented, almost. I suppose a bringer of bad news will almost always talk in clichés: clichés are protective, and they're meant to be easily understood. 'Something terrible has happened,' Mrs Coleridge said, leaning against the wall and looking as if someone had pushed her. 'You're mother has had an accident.' My response was peculiar. I said 'I know'—though of course I didn't. What I meant was that, like most people, I'd always feared the worst for those I loved the best. It wasn't until the next day that I discovered exactly what had happened. Jumping a ditch out of a wood, my mother's horse had stumbled and thrown her forward over its shoulder, knocking her hat off. She clung on as the horse galloped across most of a field, and when she eventually fell, it was onto a concrete farm track. She was knocked unconscious. My brother was in front of her. The first he knew that something was wrong was her horse careering past him, riderless.

I don't know who looked after Kit, but someone somehow called an ambulance and my mother was taken to hospital. My father arrived soon afterwards, and was told by the doctors that the fall had made a bloodclot form on her brain. If they didn't operate, she would die. If they did operate, she might live, but possibly with serious brain damage. What did he want them to do? It must have sounded like a choice, but my father realised there wasn't a choice really. If she had a chance of living, of course they must operate. She was cut out of her clothes, her head shaved, and the bloodclot was removed. A piece of her brain broke away with it.

I don't imagine that Mrs Coleridge knew how close my mother was to death. She said she'd been told that I was to carry on with the evening as planned. So while my mother was coming out of the operating theatre, Caroline and I were sitting in the back of her mother's car being driven to the dance. Caroline held my hand—but of course now everything was changed. I'd been turned from someone courting into someone being consoled. And because I had no idea myself of how ill my mother was, my distress was nowhere near as absolute as it would otherwise have been. What I really felt was confused, and conscious of suddenly being conspicuous. Throughout the dance I was aware of people pointing me out through the dusky light, and explaining. 'Yes. Isn't it awful. . . .' This made me desperate to be by myself; any sort of contact with other people felt like a betrayal. Caroline sat on my knee, late in the evening, no doubt meaning only to be kind, but I slid her off. And when the party finally ended, and we drove back to her house, I said good-night to her in the kitchen, half ran upstairs to my room, locked the door, lay on my bed fully clothed, and instantly fell asleep. I couldn't bear to be awake any longer.

*

Next morning I caught the early bus. More snow had fallen overnight, and it was bitingly cold: every time the bus stopped, and the automatic doors hissed open, a rush of freezing air reached the top deck, where I was sitting in the front seat staring through the window. I looked for signs that everything was going to be all right—two magpies for joy; the letters of a car-number which could be made into an assuaging word.

I was home by lunch and found not only Kit waiting, but also my grandmother (my mother's mother). Kit and I immediately shut ourselves in our parents' bedroom, and he told me about the accident: how it had happened; how the doctors didn't expect her to live; how my father thought we shouldn't see her, but would be staying in the hospital himself until things were clearer. For the first time I realised that the story we were caught up in was a tragic one. Also for the first time, I discovered that tragedy is seldom allowed to exist in a pure and rarefied form. Life's little ironies keep breaking in on it, threatening to turn it into black comedy. When Kit and I eventually came downstairs, to the meal that my grandmother had made for us, it seemed gross even to think about food—worse still to want it. My grandmother had tied the leash of her mad, obstreperous terrier, Janey, to a leg of the dining-room table. Whenever Janey —hungry herself—went on one of her surging little bids for a snack, the table was dragged several inches across the carpet.

I think it was almost a week before my father came home from the hospital. Kit and I were standing in the hall. We hadn't put the lights on yet, so it was almost dark. When the front door opened, my father was silhouetted against a slab of grey sky, taking his hat off, and wiping his shoes on the mat. He didn't notice us in the shadow, and during that short time between the door opening and us stepping forward, we saw what he would always be too mindful of our feelings to show readily again: exhaustion, and an infinite unhealing sadness.

Almost all the rest of my mother's life seems still to exist in the present tense. My father, brother and I don't go in together to see her until several days later. It takes forty minutes to drive from home to the hospital—a little longer this first time because the roads are icy. Halfway there we have to stop for traffic lights at some roadworks, and we draw up beside a man cutting and laying a hedge. As far as he has got, the hedge is an intricate woven lattice, the sliced branches showing the yellow of egg yolks; ahead of him it is bushily chaotic. He grins at us when he sees us watching him. 'One of the old craftsmen,' my father says, and Kit and I agree.

When we reach the hospital there is that smell of medicine and lino (it is blue marbled lino), and we climb a flight of surprisingly elaborate Victorian stairs to my mother's room. My father goes in first, and Kit and I peer through the small glass window in her door, but we can't see her. When we eventually follow him, we can still hardly see her: the room is so small, and there are so many distractions. There are the flowers we have sent, and the cards. There are tubes and wires snaking across the floor so we have to step carefully. And we have to speak up, because there is a tall chipped-grey oxygen cylinder in the corner, which hisses. A flaccid tube leads from its nozzle to a mask on my mother's face.

My father has prepared us so carefully for the visit, but it's been almost impossible to know what to expect. I think Kit and I believe that our presence will have some miraculous curative effect. We have had no understanding of how far away she is from everyone and everything. She is propped up on a lumpy bank of pillows, arms stretched straight down outside the blankets. There is a plastic bracelet on one, with her name inside it. She is wearing something white—it must be a nightdress, but it looks more like a straitjacket. Her face is obscure behind the mask, but what we can see doesn't resemble her. Her shaved head has now grown a stubble, the hair much darker than before, and her brow and one cheek are stained by a huge ochre bruise.

My father and Kit and I arrange three chairs beside her bed, and take it in turns to sit nearest her. 'The three wise monkeys,' someone says—it's a family joke—but there's no response. We sometimes squeeze her hand and say 'If you can hear me, squeeze my hand back,' but there's no response to that either. We will do this very often over the next few months, and occasionally we will think we felt something. But my mother will stay more or less comatose for the next three years, then gradually recover her speech before dying without leaving hospital almost exactly ten years after the accident. Kit and I will grow up, make our own lives, and spend a great deal of time away from home. But my father will always be there, visiting her nearly every day, unstinting and saintly in his devotion to her.

6

ANNIVERSARIES

The Fourth

Anniversary weather: I drive
under a raw sunset, the road
cramped between drifts, hedges
polished into sharp crests.

I have it by heart now;
on this day in each year
no signposts point anywhere
but east into Essex,

and so to your ward,
where snow recovers tonight
the ground I first saw lost
four winters ago.

Whatever time might bring,
all my journeys take me
back to this dazzling dark:
I watch my shadow ahead

plane across open fields,
out of my reach for ever,
but setting towards your bed
to find itself waiting there.

The First

What I remember is not
your leaving, but your not
coming back—and snow
creaking in thick trees,

burying tracks preserved
in jagged grass below.
All afternoon I watched
from the kitchen window

a tap thaw in the yard,
oozing into its stiff sack,
then harden when evening
closed with ice again.

And I am still there,
seeing your horse return
alone to the open stable,
its rein dragging behind

a trail across the plough,
a blurred riddle of scars
we could not decipher then,
and cannot heal now.

The Second

I had imagined it all—
your ward, your shaved head,
your crisp scab struck there
like an ornament,

but not your stillness.
Day after day I saw
my father leaning forward
to enter it, whispering

'If you can hear me now,
squeeze my hand', till snow
melted in sunlight outside
then turned to winter again

and found him waiting still,
hearing the slow hiss
of oxygen into your mask,
and always turning to say

'Yes, I felt it then',
as if repeating the lie
had gradually made it true
for him, never for you.

The Third

Three years without sight,
speech, gesture, only
the shadows of clouds
shifting across your face

then blown a world away.
What sleep was that, which
light could never break?
What spellbound country

claimed you, forbidding you
even to wake for a kiss?
If it was death,
whose hands were those

warm in my own, and whose
astonishing word was it
that day when leaving
your sunlit room I heard

'Stay; stay', and watched
your eyes flick open once,
look, refuse to recognise
my own, and turn away?

The Fourth

The evening falls with snow
beginning again, halving
the trees into whiteness,
driving me with it towards

the end of another year.
What will it send for you
that this has abandoned?
You are your own survivor,

bringing me back the world
I knew, without the time
we lost; until I forget
whatever it cannot provide

I'll always arrive like this,
having no death to mourn,
but rather the life we share
nowhere beyond your room,

our love repeating itself
like snow I watch tonight,
which spins against my window
then vanishes into the dark.

A DYING RACE

The less I visit, the more I think
myself back to your elegant house
I grew up in. The drive uncurled
through swaying chestnuts discovers it
standing four square, white-
washed unnaturally clear,
as if it were shown me by lightning.

It's always the place I see,
not you. You're somewhere outside,
waving goodbye where I left you
a decade ago. I've even lost sight
of losing you now; all I can find
are the mossy steps you stood on
—a visible loneliness.

I'm living four counties away, and still
I think of you driving south each night
to the ward where your wife is living.
How long will it last?
You've made that journey six years
already, taking comparative happinesses
like a present, to please her.

I can remember the fields you pass,
the derelict pill-boxes squatting
in shining plough. If I was still there,
watching your hand push back
the hair from her desperate face,
I might have discovered by now
the way love looks, its harrowing clarity.

IN THE ATTIC

Even though we know now
your clothes will never
be needed, we keep them,
upstairs in a locked trunk.

Sometimes I kneel there,
holding them, trying to relive
time you wore them, to remember
the actual shape of arm and wrist.

My hands push down between
hollow, invisible sleeves,
hesitate, then lift
patterns of memory:

a green holiday, a red christening,
all your unfinished lives
fading through dark summers,
entering my head as dust.

WOODING

From windows in the Home, old people
stared across the park, watching us
force rhododendron branches back
and trample nettles till the cedar logs

appeared. We must have looked minute:
a father and two sons no more than silhouettes
which stooped, and staggered comically
to where a trailer stood half darkened

by the wall. It took an hour.
And afterwards, to see us fooling
round the green wet-smelling load,
they would have thought us happy.

There we were: me running, my brother
kicking leaves, and each of us decked out
with split sweet chestnut husks
as spiky nipples on our coats.

The whole short afternoon we spoke
of anything except your death,
and then, next day, beyond that
blank enormous wall we buried you,

still destitute of ways to show our grief.

THE LINES

November, and the Sunday twilight fallen
dark at four—its hard unbroken rain
battering the garden. Vacantly I fill
this first week-end alone with anything—

the radio, a paperback you never read:
In 1845 200,000 navvies, 3,000 miles of line.
Lost faces lift—*a mania, a human alligator,*
shovels clinking under high midsummer sun.

The heat-haze dances meadowsweet and may,
whole cliffs collapse, and line by line
I bring your death to lonely hidden villages,
red-tiled farms, *helpless women and timid men.*

THE HOUSE THROUGH

At the iron lodge-gates
I melt for the first time,
leaving rust unstirred,
dew gripping a slack chain.

This is the drive—
a formal line through beech
and open ground where horses
graze as ever. What if I

float close? What if then
I touch one drinking? Slow
and whiskery the warm head
looms towards me, seeing

nothing but a rim of moss
around the water-butt, trees,
and wind across the field
brushing grass to molten silver.

*

Here at the door I am
identical with its thin paint.
Then one step and darkness
falls in a furious storm

of grains, splinters, rings
until daylight appears again,
and the hall, and his voice
outside in the garden singing.

*

It is *Smoke Gets In Your Eyes*—
most of the words forgotten.
There he is, kneeling,
peering for weeds

where the flowerbed bends
in a haze of lavender.
His Sunday paper blows free,
its awkward panicking wings

flap on the lawn, but I am
more stealthy than that,
drifting behind him to watch
as obscurely as only I can.

Now I come clear for him,
slipping my miniature
into his head, wearing
my favourite green tweed skirt.

He frowns, a slow trickle
of sweat scarring his cheek,
then I flicker away, vanishing
back through the garden indoors

where I wait for him: here
on his desk is my photograph,
smiling, and here in the cupboard
my clothes, as they were before.

7

BATHING AT GLYMENOPOULO

Lotophagi. I can believe it:
first moment ashore the heat
stunned us—a lavish blast
and the stink of horses.
Then it was *Mister. Mister.
Captain McKenzie*—bathing girls
round from the beach, white
towels and parasols weaving
through gun-carriages, crates
and saddlery lined on the quay
to pelt us with flowers. *Want
Captain McKenzie? I give you
good times*. But we rode away,
eyes-front and smiling, pursued
until the Majestic gates.

Men to the grounds, officers
one to a cool high-ceilinged room—
mine with a balcony looking
down to the lake. There were pelicans
clambering carefully in and out
and in, never still, wrecking
the stagnant calm, fighting,
and shaking their throats
with a flabby rattle. Otherwise,
peace—the cedar layered
in enormous green-black slabs
and shading tents on the lawn;
the horses only a rumour—
stamping and snorting
out by the kitchen garden.

Each morning we rode early
to Christmas Hill—two hours
of dressage in dusty circuits
then home with the sun still low.
For the rest, time was our own—
no orders, no news from France,
but delicious boredom: polo
some evenings, and long afternoons
bathing at Glymenopoulo. Iras,
I have you by heart, giggling
and stumbling up from the breakers
into my photograph, one thin hand
pressed to your cheek, your knee-
length, navy-blue costume puckered
and clinging. I singled you out

day after day after day—
to swim with, to dawdle
arm in arm on the beach
as the furious sun sank, and later
to hear your pidgin whispers
dancing in waterfront cafés:
You not like anyone. Gentling
than other Captain McKenzies.
You not like others—
your lemon-smelling hair
loose and brushing my mouth,
your bracelets clinking,
and languorous slow waltzes
twirling us round and round
in the smoky half-light. *Luck.*

I kept telling myself. *Luck.*
It will end—but the lazy days
stretched into months,
and then we were riding out
on a clear pastel-blue morning
to Christmas Hill as ever.
And half-way, at Kalia,
stopped at our watering place—
a date grove fringing the pool,
and the whole troop fanned
in a crescent to drink.
I was dismounted, leading my horse
over packed sand, empty-headed
and waving flies from my face
when the firing began. Ten shots,

perhaps—flips and smacks
into date trunks or puffing the sand
and nobody hurt. But we charged—
all of us thinking *At last. Action
at last,* as our clumsy light brigade
wheeled under the trees and away
up a steady slope. I was far left,
drawing my sword with a stupid
high-pitched yelp as we laboured
through silvery mirage lakes.
They were waiting ahead—
Senussi, no more than a dozen,
their gypsy silhouettes crouching
and slinking back into stones
as we breasted the rise.

The end of the world. A sheer
wall falling hundreds of feet
to a haze of yellow scrub.
I wrenched myself round, sword
dropped, head low, to a dead
teetering halt as our line
staggered, and buckled, and broke
in a clattering slide. I can
hear it again—the panicking
whinneys, shouts, and the rush
of scree where they shambled off
into space. It has taken three days
to bury them—one for the trek
to the valley floor, one to scratch
their ranks of graves, one to return.

There is little the same. At six
we have curfew now: I am writing this
after dark, on my knee, in the School
of Instruction grounds, in a tent.
I cannot sleep—sirens disturb me,
groaning up from the harbour.
Those are the ships from Gallipoli,
unloading their trail of stretchers
to the Majestic, where you will be
waiting, Iras, I know, stopped
outside the gates, high-heeled
just as you were, with your hair
fluffed out after swimming, repeating
your tender sluttish call, *Want
Captain McKenzie? I give you good times*.

I lost one slipper going down,
the other surfacing. An officer
barefooted. Think of it.
Think of how I hung there
treading water, dizzy, scared
and shouting for my luggage—
shirts and trousers billowing
below me over sunken rope
and drowned unflinching heads.

So many still to jump. I saw
some naked, some in uniform
crawl out on deck, climb up
its tilting polished slope,
hesitate, and leap at last.
The darkness buried them,
each hopeless figure lost
for ever with those horses
screaming as the water rose.

Days away, I woke. A corridor,
the nurses, and a voice above me
saying *Alexandria. This is Alex.*
Opposite my bed two soldiers
turned to look, then crouched
above an orange box again.
Watching where a scorpion
and scuttling small tarantula
circled on their stage of leaves.

A LYRICAL BALLAD

All this was years ago, but how could I forget
the first thing I did when you finally left me
was grow distinctly unlike myself—so distinctly unlike
that when help was offered I took it. Those kind hosts

my Canadian cousins—if cousins they were, and at what
distant remove from me I no longer remember—
invited me out for a slice of their black sheep life
which had come to the good: ten luxy days in Vancouver

and ten so absurd I was wondering: am I myself
or not? *This one's the big surprise,* they told me
This one'll really leave every trouble behind—
and I found I was thousands of feet up the Rockies

expected to horse-trek. Horses! I'd sooner be called
a coward. So every morning, while they would be
tinkling and giggling and shouting goodbye in the distance
I would be left as I wanted, free to wander alone.

The mountains were everything everyone said,
but the village . . . Looked down on, it seemed that a flock
of sea gulls had landed and suddenly atrophied:
rough slate roofs like wings stuck out, white clapboard walls

mottled with green, and all deserted but ours—
ours had stayed as a holiday home for anyone
thinking they ought to refresh themselves with the sight
of a world run to seed, and a scruffy mine

which was famous, exhausted, and left to decay. The mine
itself was a ship with its side stoved in—a huge hull
criss-crossed with ladders and platforms running
wherever I chose to look, but mostly drawing me down

to a plug of dirty cement where the shaft began.
I never went close, but my morning walk to the pines,
which began where the village stopped, would show me
as much as I wanted to see. For days I imagined this

was the view that I would remember: this I decided
would float through my head when I thought of the time
I was telling myself to forget you. It seemed enough.
But just as my visit was ending, and I was up there

under the pines of a morning as usual, brooding,
someone appeared at my side who made me believe
I was wrong. He emerged from the trees with no more
than the prickly crack of needles and *Well . . . Good day . . .*

—a figure who when I was squinting up to him
into the sun, and glimpsing tangled hair, a tartan shirt,
I thought might be insane, or a beached hippy—
someone who might be expected to sell me a ring

from a tray of bent-nail jewellery. All he wanted,
in fact, was to reveal what he called *Our treasure.*
I guess you're a visitor here, he said. *Don't ever you go
without seeing this. That would be foolish.* It was an ark—

though more like a shed which might float than an ark,
a peeling, twenty-foot hulk built God knows when
by God knows who, with a red-roofed cabin on top
and room, I should have imagined, to sail no more

than a dozen normal-sized creatures away from the flood
which would or would not be coming. (Unless it was spoken
that only diminutive insects could go, in which case
thousands could live.) My friend just showed me over

and vanished, politely, running his hand in silence
over the tatty prow, so I thought he was probably
mad after all. And late through that last afternoon
I lounged in the sun with my back to the cooling hull

amazed, when I wasn't just staring down at the mine
and the misting folds of valley on valley beyond,
at what people will do to make sure they escape,
or make sure there's a chance of escaping, and live

at whatever the cost for an evening like that one
I watched coming on, with scratchy grass beneath me
and pine cones thumping into their circles of brown—
still thinking if any of these things mattered at all

it was only because I would one day describe them
to you, although you had told me already you thought
you were too far away to care—which, I should say,
I understood at the time, and have known, come to that, ever
    since.

Where the cab smashed it, ⅃AW T'NOD is my marker—
West 23rd, and a block to Joey's apartment, the manholes
spurting their usual sprays of steam. I stride them down,
blind in each cloud, then myself, then blind again.

And first thing back I phone you, the quick trampolining
bbbbrrring, bbbbrrring bouncing me thousands of miles to
                                        your desk,
your bedside, wherever I catch you. *Only a fortnight now*—
your speech is slow, as if filtered through water—*Come soon . . .*

Joey thinks he is passing the time for me, asking me *Nightcap?*—
wiping the kitchen table clean with his inside cuff
and trickling two steady tracks of cocaine. *Me first?
Or did I go first last night?* If he speaks at all after this

what he says is the same: *I never fought, but I tell you,
it fucked me up. I hid three years. I even tried
faking my death, and it must have worked. Those others,
who went, they're fucked up too, but more. Now I'm free*

and I never killed anyone. Ask around. Not a single one.
I make my excuses early, and lie on my unmade bed
telling myself I might see you, or hear your voice
in the rain of luminous atoms streaking the air.

But you never appear. When the atoms subside at last
it is only for traffic—the hiss of its surf all night,
and Joey padding the corridor barefoot just before sleep,
some almost-forgotten instinct reminding him: bolt the door.

THE GORILLA GIRL

I might have been Linnaeus in another life,
or Darwin, even. Who I think I am is Crusoe—
a sort of Crusoe back to front: a woman
up a mountain, with no prospect of the sea,
too many people, and the country that I chose
a thick familiar green on every side. Perhaps
not Crusoe, then. But still, I feel marooned.

Early evening is the best, between the curfew
and the darkness with its sudden soundless crash.
I rope my tent-flap back and idly sit—
a film director in my teak and canvas chair
(these last takes take themselves). Above the camp
the jungle clamours to begin at once—a torrent
poured across the mountain range, and frozen:
vast and featureless and always plumed with mist
as though it might be bursting into flames,
or going out. My guards all think I'm crazy,
watching it—I'm not surprised. None of them
can understand the miracles I've done, or guess,
although they call me 'The Gorilla Girl',
what being that might mean. They brought me here
for safety, but their safety was a rifle
jostling in my back, my lovely look-out post
abandoned, someone shouldering my rucksack,
and me crouching at the tail-gate of a truck,
ridiculous, a chicken cradled under either arm.
*Soon the revolution's over—some time soon—
and then we'll set you free.* They told me so
the moment we were settled in these foothills—
but I've heard them talking since, and know

the day their crackpot general reaches us
I'm earmarked as his floozie. If they win, that is.

I'm through with living in the lousy world of men
and their ambitions—but I can't escape, not easily,
at least. Although I never seemed to be escaping
in my months spent on the mountain. There was work,
of course, the sort that only zookeepers and scientists
might see. I mean, my stack of dew-stained notebooks
telling how gorillas live. More than that was something
I'm embarrassed to call 'love', but love it was,
or what I turned it into. And who wouldn't, crouched
for hours on flimsy platforms of lobelia and lichen
in the crowns of trees, not moving, hardly breathing,
imagining a glimpse was all I'd get. Imagining,
but never absolutely sure—and so lured on to days
of prowling down their musky, sopping corridors,
fern one minute, celery the next, pursuing them
—my shy, suspicious, almost-friends by now—
until the moment I had longed for. Which was just
a look: not angry, or afraid, but simply curious.
I know that everything I say sounds farcical—
or mad—and yet to meet that gaze, and hold it,
squatting by a rhododendron log, one hand tight
around a stick of rhubarb, was enough to start
the huge, involved machinery of tenderness,
and let myself be known for what I am.

As soon as darkness falls, the guards will wave me
inwards to my tent. But I won't let them do it—
I untie the flap, secure it, and turn up the stove
as if I wanted peace and nothing else.
What happens after that is always automatic:
I'll stretch out on my bed and watch the sunset

deepen into amber through my canvas, shut my eyes,
and wait for sleep to come. For hours before it does
I'm hardly here at all: the best of me is huddled
in a tree-fork taking everything as given—
how the stars blaze out from nowhere, how the leaves
appear to sizzle in the moony rain—with neither
language nor the sense to think of what in fact
obsesses me: the razor blades I've hidden in my bible;
the chipped revolver snuggling in my Kleenex pack.

ONE LIFE

Up country, her husband is working late
on a high cool veranda. His radio plays
World Service News, but he does not listen,
and does not notice how moonlight fills
the plain below, with its ridge of trees
and shallow river twisting to Lagos
a whole night's journey south. What holds
him instead are these prizes that patience
and stealthy love have caught: *papilio
dardanus*—each with the blacks and whites
of simple absolutes he cannot match.

She understands nothing of this.
Away in her distant room, she lies
too sick to see the bar-sign steadily print
its purple letters again and again on her wall,
too tired to care when the silence breaks
and this stranger, her friend, leans over the bed.
There is just one implausible thought
that haunts her as clear and perfect as ever—
the delicate pottery bowl she left
forgotten at home, still loaded with apples
and pears she knows by their English names.

Madame Livernet, our hostess, poured out the tea for her
  spaniels
each day on the dot of twelve. We must have arrived at five to:
when father's driver whisked us into the yard, what should we
  find
but an army of saucers, and Madame Livernet's bloodshot face

bowed down to the last in the line. It was easy to see at a glance
she was overflowing with love—which is why she would tell
  us *My twins*
they give me extase. And it's four times extase—can you say that?—
to have you English twins for their staying as well. We honestly
  thought

she was probably round the bend. But that didn't matter—
  from dawn
to dusk we left her alone with the dogs, and escaped to astonish
  ourselves
in what felt like the garden of Eden. It wasn't just peace after
  war—
and the glittering vineyards dipping downhill from the house,
  then climbing

from green to blue to white where the mountains began. It was
  peace
our war had never come near—no village memorials, nothing
  but kites
(I mean paper and wood) pinpricking the sky, and markets each
  week
with what until then had been pictures, or names: furious
  plums,

and nectarines banked in an avalanche always threatening to
   fall.
Anyone calling us spoilt would have spoken the truth, but no
   one
knew any better, or worse, than being like us—like children
marooned on the Lost Plateau, only there weren't the monsters.

Perhaps it was more like the Lotus Eaters . . .
If I had worries at all, they were merely from being a twin, or
   rather,
a quarter of two lots of twins. It might have been just as we
   hoped,
finding two others whose lives were hardly their own. In fact
   it was sad—

as if living in heaven meant no one could tell who you were.
How could I speak for myself? I wanted to let someone know
I worship this place. I love Madame Livernet for leaving us be;
I love her house; I love her twins; I love (I love them a bit) her dogs—

but somehow the chances never arose, or if they did, I spurned
   them.
And possibly this was as well: the morning our silky staff-car
   returned
I was ready, and simply polite—thanking Madame Livernet
   (who vanished
indoors at the run—her dogs were calling), kissing the twins,

and clutching my own twin close in the narrow back window,
watching them wave. I was thinking that if I had cried, the tears
might have doubled them up into four. We never went back,
   of course,
though every letter we promised, telling them how they were
   perfect

and meaning it, even when little by little our letters got shorter,
or lay on our desk unstamped for days, or didn't get written at
    all.
We felt, I suppose, there wasn't much further to add,
not even then—and as it is now, all I can tell is a story

of which I remember too little to make it sound more than a
    dream,
one I might wake from tomorrow, perhaps, or any day soon,
believing that if I unravelled it, then I would know what I
    wanted
from love, and why I denied it, although I can see I'd be wiser

deciphering nothing: the acres of glittering vineyards, for
    instance,
spread out on their chalky, south-facing slopes in the sun,
and the gaggle of twins, and the driver (Miller, his name was)
erupting brilliantly out of his car like a po-faced jack-in-the-box.

SOLO

For a spell, I was the singular boy
on the roof, if anyone looked. Nobody did,
so I artfully put it about that I'd caged
three dozen Almonds to please my friend.
She never once paid me a call, but I said
the Almonds would always amuse her—
their globular bodies, their tiny heads—
and should they disappear, what of the view
stretching for twenty-five miles, if a yard?
And that's not even mentioning me,
who was sure when the time was right
I'd descend, and find her on my arm:
a family man, but slipping away each night
to the roof for a talk with the birds.

That spell couldn't last. What I found
when I reached ground level were stairs
upwards again—this time to an empty loft
and a mattress thrown on the boards.
There were dust-clouds whenever you moved,
and someone had locked me in, but I knew
that a girl would appear before long
and not even ask me my name. After she'd gone
my tiredness would show she existed—that,
and the rank marigold smell. I would be left
no wiser, with only myself for company,
feasting my eyes on the gorgeous offices
catching the sunlight outside, which could be
Manhattan, or Paris, or somewhere closer to home.

Frances. You were the favoured son
they never had—a tomboy, Frankie-boy,
collar and tie through the garden gates
each early morning. *Not too far though—*

be careful. Your father's voice was the ghost
of the terrace roses, his uniform smudged
behind slithering leaves. *I promise . . .*
only as far as the road. If he could hear

he would think you meant Cairo Road,
and hopscotch in sight of the settlers'.
At eight, when his sluggish official car
ferried him down to Government House

any old chalky grid was a sign of you,
your fist-clenched, stammering dance
flicking and juddering round in his head
like a handkerchief waving goodbye.

Or so you imagine it now. Or so you say,
when you're telling me late in bed,
and sleepy enough to confuse what was
with what you're beginning to dream.

All Africa knew how the settlers behaved.
Why should he think I was safe with them?
'Cut them in half, you'll find mostly gin'
—I can hear him still—'They're out and outers.'

What did they find when the Earl was killed,
I wonder? What kind of blood did he bleed?
You were going to smile, but a sigh
catches you out, and as simply as that

you're asleep, quickly swivelling round in my arms
so it seems you are trying to shake yourself free.
I click off the light, and at once, with my eyes shut
I can see you again, crouching close at my side

when we stop on a stretch of moonlit road
and discover the Earl, whoever he was, with his head
crammed through his knees on the floor of a car,
his evening dress speckled with glass. Listen:

that's the Savoy Orpheans, foxtrotting out
from a wireless dumped on his passenger seat,
and the car itself is climbing a sandstone rock
like a toy someone pretended could dance.

It might be bad luck, we are hoping—
he's drunk. But an accident wouldn't explain
this gooey hole in the core of his ear
where you show me a bullet went in.

Not that you're with me for long. When you say
I'll go for some help. Stay put, you've already gone,
your tie like a tongue flipped over your shoulder,
leaving me wandering stupidly round and round

on worn-out grass by the car. I am guessing
There must be evidence here. Footprints?
A cartridge case? but each step I take
explodes and disperses a cloud of dust

until I can scarcely be sure which footprints
are innocent: which ones are mine,
which yours, and which, supposing any are his,
might be the killer's—and whether or not

I should pay any heed to this hoarse emphatic whisper
which says out of nowhere *Don't look in the car*
Don't look at the Earl. It's as if I were dreaming
and could not control what I saw. As if I might find

his face had been changed into one that I know,
or into my own, and could never be altered back
to a stranger's again—not even by half sitting up
in the bed beside you like this, reminding myself

I am home, completely awake, and seeing you still
with your beautiful boyish face on the pillow
masked by your hair, but clearly smiling at something
you will not remember tomorrow, which I cannot share.

ACKNOWLEDGEMENTS

'The Pleasure Steamers', 'Leaving Belfast', 'Inside And Out', 'Anniversaries', 'A Dying Race' and 'In The Attic' were first published in *The Pleasure Steamers* (Carcanet, 1978); *Independence* was published by The Salamander Press in 1981; 'Open Secrets', 'The Letter', 'Writing', 'The Great Man', 'Anne Frank Huis', 'From The Imperial', 'Beginning The Move', 'Wooding', 'The Lines', 'The House Through', 'Bathing At Glymenopoulo', 'On Dry Land', 'The Interval', 'West 23rd', 'One Life' and 'Solo' (then called 'Living With Myself') were first published in *Secret Narratives* (The Salamander Press, 1983).

Acknowledgements are due to the editors of the following magazines, in which previously uncollected poems first appeared: *The London Review of Books*, *The Observer*, *The Paris Review*, *Poetry Review* and *The Times Literary Supplement*. 'Skating' was commissioned by *Poetry Review*, and a longer version than the one printed here was published in Vol. 73, No. 3.

The source for 'The Gorilla Girl' is Dian Fossey's *Gorillas In The Mist* (Hodder & Stoughton, 1984); the source for 'Dangerous Play' is James Fox's *White Mischief* (Cape, 1982).

MORE ABOUT PENGUINS, PELICANS
AND PUFFINS

For further information about books available from Penguins please write to Dept EP, Penguin Books Ltd, Harmondsworth, Middlesex UB7 0DA.

In the U.S.A.: For a complete list of books available from Penguins in the United States write to Dept DG, Penguin Books, 299 Murray Hill Parkway, East Rutherford, New Jersey 07073.

In Canada: For a complete list of books available from Penguins in Canada write to Penguin Books Canada Ltd, 2801 John Street, Markham, Ontario L3R 1B4.

In Australia: For a complete list of books available from Penguins in Australia write to the Marketing Department, Penguin Books Australia Ltd, P.O. Box 257, Ringwood,Victoria 3134.

In New Zealand: For a complete list of books available from Penguins in New Zealand write to the Marketing Department, Penguin Books (N.Z.) Ltd, Private Bag, Takapuna, Auckland 9.

In India: For a complete list of books available from Penguins in India write to Penguin Overseas Ltd, 706 Eros Apartments, 56 Nehru Place, New Delhi 110019.